John Deere

History Maker Bios

Jane Sutcliffe

LERNER PUBLICATIONS COMPANY • MINNEAPOLIS

In memory of Bill and Irene Sutcliffe

Lerner Publications Company
A division of Lerner Publishing Group
241 First Avenue North
Minneapolis, MN 55401 U.S.A.

Website address: www.lernerbooks.com

Library of Congress Cataloging-in-Publication Data

Sutcliffe, Jane.
    John Deere / by Jane Sutcliffe ; illustrations by Big Time Attic.
    p. cm. — (History maker bios)
    Includes bibliographical references and index.
    ISBN-13: 978-0-8225-6579-6 (lib. bdg. : alk. paper)
    ISBN-10: 0-8225-6579-X (lib. bdg. : alk. paper)
    1. Deere, John, 1804-1886—Juvenile literature. 2. Deere & Company—History—Juvenile literature. 3. Industrialists—United States—Biography—Juvenile literature. 4. Agricultural machinery industry—United States—History—Juvenile literature. 5. Plows—United States—History. I. Title.
    HD9486.U62D447 2007
    338.7'6292252092—dc22 [B]   2006018508

Manufactured in the United States of America
1 2 3 4 5 6 – JR – 12 11 10 09 08 07

TABLE OF CONTENTS

INTRODUCTION

John Deere was a man with a good idea. He saw that farmers had trouble plowing through the rich, sticky soil of the prairies. So the young blacksmith came up with a new kind of plow. His plow cut through the soil and turned prairie land into farmland. John worked to make his plow better until it was the favorite of farmers everywhere. He turned his good idea into a successful company. In time, his company—and his name—became known all around the world.

This is his story.

1

THE BOY IN THE BLACKSMITH SHOP

John Deere. The name makes people think of farms and plows and big green tractors. But John Deere didn't grow up on a farm. And he certainly never rode a tractor. When he was growing up, farmers used horses to pull the equipment on farms.

John was born February 7, 1804, in Rutland, Vermont. When he was still little, his parents moved the family to Middlebury. They opened a tailor shop there. They made clothing for the well-to-do people of the town. They worked hard. But there never seemed to be enough money to care for John and his five brothers and sisters.

John didn't grow up in a farming family. But he would have seen the types of plows farmers in Vermont used. Farmers guided the plows by hand. They used horses for extra power.

Then one day, when John was about four, the Deeres received exciting news. John's father was to receive some money from a relative in Great Britain. All he had to do was go there to collect it. So Mr. Deere kissed his wife and children good-bye and sailed away across the ocean.

John's father left for Great Britain in the early 1800s. A journey across the Atlantic Ocean could be dangerous.

And that was the last the family ever saw of Mr. Deere. No one knows what happened. Perhaps the ship was attacked by pirates. Perhaps it sank in a storm. Whatever happened, John spent the rest of his childhood without a father.

He grew up without much money too. Mrs. Deere stitched and sewed. But money was tighter than ever. When he was old enough, John got a job after school to help out.

John's mother tried to make extra money through her tailoring business.

John got a job in a blacksmith shop like this one. Blacksmiths were important members of their communities.

Then, when he was seventeen, he was done with school. He found a job in Benjamin Lawrence's blacksmith shop. This was an important job. John learned to make all kinds of things made of iron—everything from pots and pans to horseshoes.

Little by little, John discovered the secret of shaping metal. He learned to heat the iron until it was just right. Then he used a hammer and his own strength to work the iron into the shape he wanted. John learned fast. Before long, the other smiths were nodding and whispering that young John Deere did fine work.

So That's What That Means

John learned to heat a piece of iron until it was glowing bright yellow. Then it was hot enough to shape with his hammer. He had to work fast, though, before the iron cooled again. He learned to "strike while the iron was hot." In time, others started using that saying too. They meant, "Take advantage of an opportunity before it's gone."

John met
Demarius
Lamb and
fell in love
with her.

After four years in Benjamin Lawrence's
shop, John had learned all he could. He
had become a young man. He was tall,
with wide shoulders and bright red hair.
And he was in love. He had met a young
woman with the unusual name of
Demarius Lamb. It was time for John to
think about his future.

One day, a man came to see John. He owned a big, new sawmill. The mill would turn giant logs into finished boards. It was going to need all kinds of iron parts to make it run. And the owner wanted John to make the parts—*all* the parts.

John was delighted. For the first time, he was working on his own. The job didn't last long. But when it was over, he knew one thing. He would own his own blacksmith shop someday.

Sawmills churned out lumber used for buildings in the quickly growing United States. John was asked to make the iron parts for one of these sawmills in Vermont.

He made another big decision too. In January 1827, he and Demarius were married. By that summer, their first baby was on the way.

John was going to have a family to support. He knew there wouldn't be enough money to set up his own shop— at least just yet. His dream would have to wait.

2 THE WANDERING BLACKSMITH

The Deeres never stayed in one place for very long. They traveled from one Vermont town to another. John worked for one blacksmith after another. But he was restless. What he really wanted was his own blacksmith shop.

By 1829, John decided it was time to open his own shop. There was only one problem. He had no money. So John borrowed the money from a man named Jay Wright and promised to pay him back later.

At last, John had his own shop! It was in a place called Four Corners in the town of Leicester. John quickly made a name for himself for the fine ironwork he did. Farmers especially prized the iron tools he made. They said his hay forks were so finely polished that "they slipped in and out of hay like needles."

John made farm tools and other items out of iron in his first blacksmith shop.

Blacksmiths worked with fire and heated metal. Fire was a constant danger to shop owners. John's blacksmith shop in Vermont (ABOVE) caught fire twice.

Then the worst possible thing happened. John woke one night to find that his blacksmith shop was on fire! He watched as the flames destroyed his dream. John borrowed more money from Mr. Wright. Once again, he built his shop.

But fires were common in blacksmith shops. And luck was not on John's side. Once again, his shop caught fire. He was able to borrow a bit more money from Mr. Wright. But his shop was gone.

Villiagers in the 1800s gather to watch a blacksmith at work. John's work took him and his family from town to town.

Now John had no shop and no job. And he owed money. It was time to move again. John found a new job with good pay in Royalton. His new boss even let the Deeres live in a house that he owned.

Demarius must have hoped that this time they'd be staying for good. But John was not happy. He still wanted his own blacksmith shop. After only two years, the Deeres were off to a new town.

This time, it was the town of Hancock. John set up a blacksmith shop there and went to work. Once more, the iron tools he made were a favorite among the area's farmers. But then a strange thing happened. There were fewer and fewer farmers around.

Where had all the farmers gone? They had packed up and headed west. Hard times had come to Vermont. Many farmers had trouble paying their bills. The farmers moved to places like Ohio or Illinois to make a new start. A new start must have sounded good to John too.

A covered wagon carries its passengers westward to Ohio in the 1800s. Many farmers left Vermont for the Midwest.

Then suddenly, things got even worse for the Deeres. All this time, Jay Wright had been waiting for John to repay the money he'd borrowed. Finally, Mr. Wright got tired of waiting. He wanted his money. If John couldn't pay, he'd go to jail!

That helped John make up his mind fast. He had heard that the town of Grand Detour, Illinois, needed a blacksmith. That settled the matter. He would go west. He would have to pay the money back later.

As communities in Illinois began growing, many were in need of blacksmiths. John took the opportunity to move to Grand Detour, Illinois (SHOWN ABOVE).

He had to leave his family behind. By then, John and Demarius had four children, and a fifth was on the way. They would have to join him later.

In November 1836, John packed up his tools. Then he kissed his family good-bye. At thirty-two, he was headed to Grand Detour.

THE LONG WAY WEST

John's trip could not have been easy. First, he had to travel by stagecoach, then by boat, then by bumpy wagon across the prairie. The journey took weeks. And he was probably homesick for his family the whole time.

3 THE SINGING PLOW

J ohn was a busy man from the moment he arrived in Grand Detour. He barely had time to build his shop. A mill owner needed a broken part repaired. Farmers needed him to mend tools or make brand new ones.

Suddenly John was heating and hammering and shaping iron from before sunrise until after sunset. He worked seven days a week. He had never been this busy.

Like John, many of the farmers in Grand Detour were from New England. They had left behind the rocky New England soil for the rich soil of the prairie. The prairie soil was more fruitful. But it was also terribly sticky.

John worked long, hard hours in his blacksmith shop in Grand Detour.

John wanted to make a better plow so farmers wouldn't have to scrape off the sticky mud.

Each spring, the farmers plowed their fields to break up the soil and get it ready for planting. That soil stuck to the iron plows like paste. Everyone said it was enough to make folks turn around and go back to New England.

In his shop, John couldn't help hearing the farmers' grumbling. He knew that a cast-iron plow would never be made smooth enough to keep the soil from sticking to it. Still, he wondered if he could make a plow that would help.

One day, John was in the town sawmill. He noticed a broken steel saw blade that had been tossed in a corner. That gave him an idea. He asked the owner if he could have the blade. Then he went to work.

First, he cut the sharp teeth off the blade. He heated the steel and hammered it into just the shape he wanted. He attached it to a large piece of iron. Then he dug up a young tree and carved it into two crude handles. When John was done, he was looking at a very rough plow with a shiny steel blade.

Sawmills used smooth, sharp-toothed steel blades like these to cut lumber. John saw a use for the steel blades and set to work using one to make a plow blade.

He set his plow by the front door of his shop and waited. A few days later, a farmer spotted the new plow. He asked John who had made it.

John replied that he made it himself, woodwork and all.

The farmer looked the plow over. It certainly looked as though it would work, he told John. He offered to take the plow home and try it. If it worked, he would keep it and pay for it. If not, he would return it.

John used a steel blade to make his first plow (SHOWN BELOW).

Farmers tried John's new steel-bladed plow. They were thrilled that it sliced cleanly through the soil.

John agreed. Sure enough, two weeks later, the farmer was back—without the plow. It had worked just as John had hoped. The steel blade had sliced through that sticky soil and come out clean again.

Of course, John knew that he was not the first to come up with a steel plow. Others had had the same idea. But their plows always seemed to have some problem. John was determined to make his plow a success.

But his new plow would have to wait until he found a way to get more steel. Besides, John had something else on his mind. In 1838, his family had at last arrived in Grand Detour. Demarius must have been happy when she saw the fine house John had built. It meant they were in Grand Detour to stay.

John built this house in Grand Detour for his family. He added on to it as his family grew.

A Family Tale

A Deere family story says that John ran to meet his family when they arrived in Grand Detour. Demarius was carrying the baby son he had never seen. "Here John, you hold him a while," she told him. "I've carried him all the way from Vermont."

Morning to night, John worked in his shop. He managed to find enough steel to make two more plows that year. The next year, he made ten. He sharpened and polished each one until it hummed as it slipped through the soil. Soon folks were calling it "the singing plow."

By 1842, John was making a hundred singing plows a year. It looked like that sticky soil was going to be very good luck for John.

4 MOLINE

Better! That word must have echoed in John's head morning, noon, and night. He was always looking for a way to make his plows better.

He talked to the farmers who used his plows in their fields. He listened to their suggestions for improvements. Then he went back to his shop to turn good ideas into better plows.

Often he barely even stopped to eat. A visitor to the Deere home said that John "would come to his meals with his hat in his hand, put his hat on the floor beside him, eat, put on his hat and return to the shop."

John was looking to the future. Then suddenly, someone from his past found him. Jay Wright hadn't given up trying to get the money John still owed him. He went to court in Illinois to force John to pay. And this time, John had the money. When the debt was repaid, John had one less thing to worry about.

John kept busy working in his blacksmith shop in Grand Detour.

To keep up with the demand for his plows, John had to build a bigger factory. To do so, he got help from his new business partner, Leonard Andrus (LEFT).

By 1843, John wanted to make his plow business not just better. He wanted to make it bigger. So John took on a partner named Leonard Andrus. They built a two-story factory about a block from John's blacksmith shop. John had steel delivered to his factory all the way from Great Britain.

John wasn't always good with the money side of the business. So in 1846, he hired his eighteen-year-old son, Albert, as a bookkeeper. He was looking forward to having Albert join him in the business. Then, just a year later, Albert suddenly fell ill and died.

Grand Detour didn't seem the same without Albert. John had already been thinking of moving. Roads around Grand Detour were often bad. There was no railroad. That made it difficult for John to have steel shipped in and plows shipped out.

In 1848, when he was forty-four, John left Mr. Andrus behind and moved his business seventy-five miles away to Moline, Illinois. The town was right on the Mississippi River. Big riverboats brought in all the steel that John needed. They left loaded with John's plows.

John moved his business to Moline, Illinois, on the banks of the Mississippi River.

OOPS!

John had some fancy bricks put on his factory as decoration. They were supposed to say 1848, the year the factory was built. Instead, when the job was done, they read 1847. It was too late to do anything about the mistake. So John just started telling people that the factory had been built in 1847.

John had his business where he wanted it. That June, he took on two new partners, Robert Tate and John Gould. By July, the new plow factory was being built. And by September, the company had finished its first ten plows.

Soon John's factory was turning out one thousand plows a year. Still, he had never stopped trying to make his plows better too. He was always making one improvement or another. "I will never put my name on a product that does not have in it the best that is in me," he liked to say.

But John's partners thought their plows were just fine the way they were. They didn't see why John had to tinker with them. When John said "better," his partners said "good enough." Back and forth, the argument would go. At last, in 1852, after four years, the partners split up.

John watches a farmer using one of his plows. John always wanted to improve his plows. His business partners did not agree.

John wasn't on his own for long though. Just two years later, his sixteen-year-old son, Charles, joined the business. Even though Charles was young, he was a fast learner. He quickly went from bookkeeper's helper to salesman to manager. He was good with the money matters that John found so difficult.

In 1856, John made Charles a partner in the business. Maybe at last, he had found the perfect partner for his company.

5 THE PLOW KING

The newspaper ad read, "Plows! Plows! Plows!" There was no doubt what John Deere was selling. By the mid-1850s, his factory was turning out fourteen thousand plows a year. No wonder a reporter called John the Plow King.

John wanted to make sure people everywhere knew about his company. He went to dozens of county and state fairs. He talked about his plows and showed how they worked. He entered plow contests—and won. His hard work paid off. Soon he was one of the largest plow makers in the country.

John's little company had certainly grown! Charles had done his part to help make the company successful too. John was proud that his son was turning out to be a good businessman. As time passed, he let Charles run more and more of the business.

John's son Charles Deere (RIGHT) took over more of his father's business.

In the Moline factory, water from the Mississippi helped provide power to turn the grinding and polishing wheels.

Of course, John wasn't ready to quit altogether. He still helped make important decisions for the company. He never stopped thinking of ways to make his company and his plows better. Once in a while, he even worked in the shop alongside his employees.

All those plows had made John a very wealthy man. At last, he and Demarius were able to enjoy the life for which they had worked so hard.

A VOICE FOR FREEDOM

In 1861, the Civil War began. Soldiers from Southern states battled soldiers from Northern ones. Slavery was one of the reasons for the war. John began speaking out against slavery. Some people thought his words were too forceful. But John believed that all people should be free. And he wasn't afraid to say so.

Then in 1865, Demarius died. John went back to Vermont for a time. He wanted to be with family and old friends. He struck up a close friendship with Demarius's sister, Lucenia. In May 1867, the two were married. John brought his new wife back to Moline.

With Charles in charge of the business, John had plenty of money and time to try something new. He bought a large farm and raised cattle and pigs. He also gave money to the town he loved so much to build libraries, schools, and churches.

John married Lucenia two years after his first wife, Demarius, died.

John decided he wanted to do even more for Moline. In 1873, when he was sixty-nine, he ran for mayor of Moline and won. John wasn't always a popular mayor. But he worked hard to make the town better. He built a park. He put in streetlights, sidewalks, and sewers. And he had never forgotten how terrible fire could be. He made sure Moline had a proper fire department ready at all hours.

John spent two years serving Moline as its mayor. By then, he was tired and he was often sick. It was time to let someone else run the town. He retired to the grand house he'd had built, overlooking his company. His employees often stopped by to visit him.

John was the mayor of Moline when this photograph was taken.

On May 17, 1886, at the age of eighty-two, John Deere died. His funeral was the biggest Moline had ever seen. More than four thousand people turned out to say good-bye.

There was even a plow made of flowers with the name "John Deere" written across it. That seemed like just the right honor for the man who had made plows his life. John had earned his place in history as the man who had helped tame the prairies of the Midwest. He was America's Plow King.

TIMELINE

In the year . . .

1806   John moved to Middlebury, Vermont.

1821   he began work as a blacksmith.   Age 17

1827   he married Demarius Lamb.

1828   his son Albert was born.

1829   John opened his first blacksmith shop in Leicester, Vermont.

1830   his daughter Jeannette was born.

1832   his daughter Ellen was born.

1833   he opened his second blacksmith shop in Hancock, Vermont.

1834   his daughter Frances was born.

1836   he moved to Grand Detour, Illinois.   Age 32

1837   his son Charles was born in March.
John made his first steel plow.

1840   his daughter Emma was born.

1842   his son Hiram was born.

1844   Hiram died.
John's daughter Alice was born.

1848   Albert died in January.
John moved his business to Moline, Illinois, in July.   Age 44

1851   Frances died.
John's daughter Mary was born and died a short time later.

1853   his son Charles joined the business.

1856   Charles became a partner in the business.

1865   Demarius died.

1867   John married Lucenia Lamb.

1873   he became mayor of Moline.   Age 69

1886   he died on May 17.   Age 82

JOHN DEERE

After John died, his company kept growing. New factories were built. New kinds of tools were made. In 1918, the company started making tractors too. Soon tractors became the company's biggest-selling product. In time, those tractors could be found on farms all over the world.

On each big green tractor were nine yellow letters: JOHN DEERE. It was a way of reminding everyone of the man who had started the company so long ago.

And to think that it all began with a broken saw blade and a good idea.

FURTHER READING

Bare, Margaret Ann. *John Deere, Blacksmith Boy.* New York: Macmillan Publishing Co., 1987.
This book offers readers a colorful description of the childhood and youth of John Deere.

Collins, David R. *Pioneer Plowmaker: A Story about John Deere.* Minneapolis: Carolrhoda Books, Inc., 1990.
In this book, the author tells the story of John Deere's life, for readers aged nine to twelve.

Fradin, Dennis. *Illinois.* Chicago: Children's Press, 1991.
Read this title to find more information on the history, geography, and famous people of the state of Illinois.

WEBSITES

John Deere Historic Site
http://www.deere.com/en_US/attractions/historicsite/index.html
This website has information on visiting John's home and a replica of his shop.

"The Women in John Deere's Life." John Deere.
http://www.deere.com/en_US/compinfo/student/DemariusDeerebio.html
Visit this site to read the story of John's wife and family.

BIBLIOGRAPHY

Broehl, Wayne G., Jr. *John Deere's Company: A History of Deere and Company and Its Times.* New York: Doubleday & Company, 1984.

Dahlstrom, Neil, and Jeremy Dahlstrom. *The John Deere Story: A Biography of Plowmakers John and Charles Deere.* DeKalb: Northern Illinois University Press, 2005.

Dies, Edward Jerome. *Titans of the Soil: Great Builders of Agriculture.* Chapel Hill: University of North Carolina Press, 1949.

Deere & Company. "The Story of John Deere." *John Deere.* January 2006. http://www.deere.com/en_US/compinfo /history/index.html (August 4, 2006).

Watson, Aldren. *The Village Blacksmith.* Exp. ed. New York: Cromwell, 1977.

INDEX

Acknowledgments

For photographs and artwork: : Courtesy Deere & Company, pp. 4, 12, 23, 24, 28, 32, 33, 35, 38, 39, 41, 42, 45; © Dover Publications, Inc., pp. 7, 9, 27; The Mariners Museum, Newport News, Va., p. 8; © Bettmann/CORBIS, p. 10; North Wind Picture Archives, pp. 11, 18, 19; © MPI/Hulton Archive/Getty Images, p. 13; The Granger Collection, New York, p. 16; From the JD Heritage collection, p. 17; Courtesy of the Schingoethe Center for Native American Cultures, Aurora University, p. 20; Library of Congress (LC-USZC4-3266), p. 21; © Kean Collection/Hulton Archive/Getty Images, p. 25; Photo by Hugh Talman Smithsonian Institution, p. 26; © Max W. Hunn/SuperStock, p. 31. Front cover: Courtesy Deere & Company. Back cover: The Granger Collection, New York.

For quoted material: p. 16, Wayne G. Broehl Jr., *John Deere's Company: A History of Deere and Company and Its Times* (New York: Doubleday & Company, 1984); pp. 29, 31, "The Women in John Deere's Life," Deere & Company, n.d., http://www .deere.com/en_US/compinfo/student/DemariusDeerebio.html (August 8, 2006); p. 34, Deere & Company, "The Story of John Deere," *John Deere*, January 2006, http://www.deere.com/en_US/compinfo/history/index.html (August 4, 2006).